53

Brooks B. Robinson

For the generations to come

Preface

As part of preparatory notes for this monograph we concluded: Lack of concern about the future places us where we are today. We used to have vision.

Careful consideration of the latter statement proves true. At the beginning of football or basketball season, ask any young Afrodescendant boy who loves sports concerning who is going to win the NFL or NBA championships and you can be assured that he has a vision. He will not only tell you which team he expects to win the championships, but he will also tell you the reasons why his expected outcome may not materialize. He has a vision, and he knows what is likely to disrupt his favored outcome.

Ask that same boy concerning the plight of Black Americans, he will likely say, "I don't know." Ask him about past Afrodescendant leaders who have assisted Black Americans in achieving their current state, and he will be able to name a few. The important point is that, when it comes to our past, we have fairly good grounding. However, when it comes to the future, we take time to explore mundane futures, but we take little time to consider the most important future—the plight of our people during future generations.

This monograph is intended to help readers consider important aspects of Black America's future to determine where we are likely to come out. Of course, we will attempt to identify the various factors that will help determine the possible futures. Inevitably, it is up to each of us to take the time to plot our future course, and our individual futures will combine to produce our joint future.

Foreword

What does the number "53" have to do with the future of Black Americans? If we take the digits singly, we know that the number "5" symbolizes an unelevated human nature; we have five senses and we have five appendages on or hands and feet. The number "3," on the other hand symbolizes the divine. Especially in the Christian context, we say: Father, Son, and Holy Ghost. The number "3" may also be considered as an indicator of three levels of a pyramid. In the Islamic tradition, the human is viewed as having three stages of development in terms of the ego: (transliterating here) *Nafs-i-ammara* (the basic human being with a tendency toward lust and materialism); *Nafs-i-lawwama* (the rational human that recognizes spiritual failings, a self-accusing spirit); and *Nafs-i-mutma inna* (a spirit without a pointed ego and at peace with the will of God). This framework may have informed Sigmund Freud's three-part personality structure: The id, the ego, and the super ego.

If you are a sports fan, you might recall a favorite athlete who wore or wears the number "53." For example, you might think of the 1974 Super Bowl winning Miami Dolphins under Coach Don Shula, who ran a superb defense known as the "53," which was named after #53 linebacker Bob Matheson. He would be brought in as a fourth linebacker in third down situations to rush the passer or drop back into pass coverage.

Historically, we can think of "53" as the year (1953) when the Korean War ended, and marked the beginning of the U.S. failure to win clear-cut military victories.

If we desired to be really esoteric, we could note that 5 plus 3 equals 8, which when turned on its side represents the symbol for infinity (∞). Could it be that the "53" analysis helps set the stage for our future—out to infinity?

One might adopt one of many perspectives in attempting to interpret this number "53." We have one main interpretation of the number, which we plan to use in building this monograph about Black America's future. As you read the Introduction and subsequent chapters, you will come into the full knowledge of this number and what it means for Afrodescendants' development into the future. We believe that the number best symbolizes an analytical framework that allows us to systematically examine where Afrodescendants are today, and how we might best move forward through the 21st century and beyond.

Table of Content

Chapter 1.—Introduction

Nations, states (provinces), cities (municipalities) have long-term (strategic) plans. Most firms have short- and long-term business plans. Organizations of almost any ilk have plans for their future. So why is it impossible to find a well-crafted strategic plan for Black Americans? Yes, it entails a considerable amount of work, but given the resources that are available to certain Black organizations, it seems reasonable that they would develop and publish a long-term strategic plan for Black Americans.

A starting point for developing such a plan is to perform an assessment (collect data) to characterize the status quo—where we are today. Having that information in hand, plus forecasts of future conditions enables the development of a plan that begins with preferred end states, includes a set of strategic actions that will help move us from where we are over time to our preferred end states, and it should include a mechanism for periodic assessments and course corrections. This is not rocket science. What we know is that, "If you don't know where you are going, then any road will take you there."

Having searched and having not found a solid plan for Afrodescendants' future, we were led to prepare this monograph, which provides inputs for an original assessment and forecasts for the future. All that is needed in combination with this monograph is a process to determine our future goals (end states) and a solid strategy can be developed to help us arrive at those goals (end states).

We have selected key variables for the current-period assessment and forecasts: Population, employment,

1

income, entrepreneurship, educational attainment, criminal justice, and health. A look at statistics that are associated with these variables in present-day and future contexts is sufficient to help us comprehend where we are likely to end up if the status quo is maintained.

However, Black America is not monolithic and it is not static—it is dynamic. Therefore, it is wise to have a dynamic framework within which to conduct the assessment and forecast process. In considering such a framework, we consulted one who was familiar with "futures science." The idea came forth to consider Black America's future within a "Four Alternative Futures" framework. This framework would allow us to imagine the future of Black Americans under four scenarios: Continuation, Collapse, Disciplined, and Transformational.

Under the Continuation scenario, the expectation would be that Afrodescendants would essentially grow as a group going forward—mainly using traditional methods of growth. The Collapse scenario is self-explanatory; for whatever reason, we would envision Black America as falling apart, shrinking in population, or possibly even disappearing. In the Disciplined scenario, Black Americans would return to some previously followed conservative agenda in charting our future; e.g., falling into a heavily spiritual or religious paradigm in plotting our course. Finally, the Transformational scenario would find Afrodescendants adopting currently unknown approaches to evolving our future—probably high-tech methods for organizing, planning, and developing our society in an advanced way.

While these four scenarios offer important and reasonable options for building or imagining Black America's future, another—yet related—framework came to mind for this purpose. In fact, this framework forms the basis for the title of this monograph, *53*. The framework is symbolized by Figure 1.

5		3
Do Nothing		
Accelerate Integration		Lower Class
Resegregate		Middle Class
Diaspora		Upper Class
Nation Formation		

Figure 1.—The Components of 53

Figure 1 shows five actions and three classes of persons. They represent the present and future Black American experience. Considering the classes first, clearly Black America has evolved into a class-based society. We know generally that 25% of Black Americans live in poverty (lower class). Actually, it is reasonable to place the poverty line for a family of four that includes two children under 18 years of age at about $25,000 (lower-class). It is also reasonable to say that upper-class Blacks are those that have household income above $100,000. Accordingly, middle-class Blacks would be those with incomes that fall within the lower- and upper-class ($25,001 - $99,999).[1]

Now let us consider the five actions. In Chapter 3, as we consider the future, Black America's options include, but may not be limited to: Doing Nothing, Accelerating the racial Integration process, Resegregating, promulgating a Diaspora, or taking the bold step of Nation Formation. If

---

[1]A September 2010 report from the U.S. Census Bureau entitled, *Income, Poverty, and Health Insurance Coverage in the United States: 2009*, conveys the following average distribution of income for Black alone by the income categories just cited: About 39% for lower-class, about 10% for upper-class, leaving a residual of 51% for the middle-class.

you are familiar with our writings, then you will know that we favor the latter action set for the future.[2]

This "53" framework guides our thinking and judgment as we extend statistics for the aforementioned seven variables out into the future. Our plan is to begin with a conservative, status quo trend forecast as fulfilling the "Do Nothing" action. We will then modify that status quo forecast by taking into account the roles of the three classes of Black Americans with respect to each prospective action. Consider Figure 2 in this regard:

Do Nothing	Forecast is equivalent to the status quo trend
Accelerate Integration	Likely involves upper-middle and upper income class population (weighted effect)
Resegregate	Likely involves lower-middle and lower class population (weighted effect)
Diaspora	Likely involves upper-middle class population (weighted effect)
Nation Formation	Likely involves lower-middle and lower class population (weighted effect)

Figure 2—Method for accounting for 53 in forecasts

The methodology outlined in Figure 2 will be used with respect to each of seven key series that we have identified: Population, income, employment, entrepreneurship, education, criminal justice, and health. Of course, in addition to our weighted adjustments of the status quo forecasts, we plan to incorporate available information about future trends that Afrodescendants might experience.

---

[2] Our most important contribution on "nation formation" appears in *Chosen: Black America's Calling*. However, we have also written on the topic in the remaining two books of a trilogy: *Choice: Black America's Decision* and *Change: Black America's Religion*. All three works are available at www.BlackEconomics.org.

4

At the conclusion of Chapter 3 after we have developed and discussed forecasts of the seven key series to 2050, we will be able to assess the Black American condition under the five action scenarios. The scenarios that are most favorable should be transparent by viewing the forecasts. That is not to say that we expect all Black Americans to opt for the most favorable mix of scenarios. Remember, the class structure guarantees that certain scenarios will appear more advantageous to one class versus another or some subset thereof. However, given the forecast results, Black Americans can begin to conduct the types of informed discussions that can guide our decision-making for our long-term future. In other words, we should be able to use the Chapter 3 analysis to establish end states for the year 2050, and then develop a strategy for reaching those end states.

But before rushing to the Chapter 3 analysis, let us provide context for an end state that might be revealed by that analysis. Assume for the sake of argument that we find the most favorable outcomes for Afrodescendants are associated with a nation formation effort. Would that be alarming? Should it be? Chapter 2 builds on this idea by presenting evidence concerning selected and better-known Afrodescendant nation formation and independent living efforts in the U.S. If you know your history, you will be familiar with the five nation formation efforts that we recount, which transpired on a pre-20th century basis. You may also be familiar with the three independent living cases that we cite. Here again, we stick with our "53" theme. However, we augment this 5-3 set with two additional cases of 20th century nation formation efforts.

This monograph does not contain a concluding chapter because it recounts the past, assesses the current state, and provides forecasts as a beginning for shaping our future. It provides some of the raw material that is required to fashion a long-term strategic plan for Afrodescendants. The conclusion must be written by those who take this raw material and use it to develop such a plan.

Afrodescendants are told that we were brought to North America from Africa. We did not ask to come here. For nearly four hundred years we were told what to do in America. Now America is finding it difficult to sort out its own national, state, and local affairs given its ongoing fiscal crisis. Therefore, it makes common sense, that, to the extent that we are free enough to think and plan for ourselves and given the talent that exists within our community, we should begin to plan our own future.

One day—and it may be sooner than we think—we may find that America is not able to look after us any longer. The Most Honorable Elijah Muhammad warned us of these circumstances.[3] If we have acted wisely, then we will be proud on that day because we would have looked out for ourselves. If we are fortunate, we will be able to use that plan to ensure our safety and security for the next century and beyond. By so doing, we would have preserved the best that Africa had to offer 400 years ago, and we would have preserved a nation that has an important role to play in the future history of the world.[4]

---

[3] See Elijah Muhammad's (1965), *Message to the Blackman in America*, Secretarius MEMPS Publications, Phoenix, AZ.

[4] In our aforementioned trilogy (see footnote 2), it is suggested that the American experience has prepared Afrodescendants to be the "peace makers" for the world. This is critical at a time when technology is sufficient to meet the needs of the world's population, but animus between nations and religions could threaten to destroy our world. Black Americans, with our great experience at negotiating for peace, should be able to prevent the world from going over the feared precipice of very violent (possibly nuclear) wars.

Chapter 2.--A Brief History of Afrodescendant Nation Formation and Independent Living Efforts

Arguably, American chattel slavery is synonymous with the conversion of Afrodescendants to Christianity. Afrodescendants, in their own subtle defiance, seized upon the story of the Biblical Hebrews to which they equated their struggle. It is logical that the portion of the Hebrew story that was most favored by the slaves was the passage that relates how Moses led his people across the Red Sea, which established conditions for entering the land of Canaan—the promised land. This event laid the framework for freedom and the establishment of the great nation of Israel with great kings and traditions.

Early in the American experience, Afrodescendants envisioned departure from slavery to some promised land and to independent living from their White masters. In keeping with our "53" theme, in this chapter we highlight five well-known pre-20th century cases (Nova Scotia, the American Colonization Society, Paul Cuffee, Denmark Vessey, and Abraham Lincoln's Chiriqui Plan) that portended an exodus of Afrodescendants to freedom from slavery, and we consider three important cases where Afrodescendants established highly independent living situations (Wilmington, North Carolina, Tulsa, Oklahoma, and Rosewood, Florida). We split these two sets of developments by discussing two special 20th century nation formation efforts. First, a Marcus Garvey effort that was designed to provide an exodus of Afrodescendants out of the Americas and back to Africa. Second, an Elijah Muhammad effort that was designed to prepare Afrodescendants religiously and economically to become independent in an area in North America but separate from the U.S. We cite one key source for each case.

These historical developments should serve as clear guidance to today's Afrodescendants that their ancestors valued their freedom highly, and concluded that the only method to achieve a more complete freedom was to exit the United States. For those Afrodescendants who tried highly independent living in Wilmington, Tulsa, and Rosewood, the message generated by the White response was, "not within these borders."

If the analysis that is presented in Chapter 3—which provides statistical evidence concerning the state of Black America by 2050—reveals that Afrodescendant conditions are not likely to change substantially under a "Do Nothing" scenario, then it seems reasonable to argue that Afrodescendants should reconsider historical efforts to exodus the U.S. and to live independently here. The message that screams down through history is that exodus could be the prescribed path. Consequently, Afrodescendants have a choice concerning their future. Only they can decide how their future history will read.

Five Pre-20th Century Nation Formation Cases

Exodus to Nova Scotia[5]

Besides those individual and small group cases of slaves escaping to Canada to live a life of freedom, the first major case of Afrodescendants exodusing the U.S. is linked to the Revolutionary War. Afrodescendants who fought alongside the British during the war were guaranteed safe passage back to Africa should the war be lost. While some of these Blacks' return to Africa was delayed via a sojourn

---

[5]Grace-Edward Galabuzi's (2006) Canada's *Economic Apartheid: The Social Exclusion of Racialized Groups in the New Century,* Canadian Scholars' Press, Toronto, Canada.

in Nova Scotia, many ultimately found their way back to Africa. Specifically, they were returned to an area that is now known as Sierra Leone.

On the other hand, certain Afrodescendants who fought with the British during the Revolutionary War, and the War of 1812 for that matter, who were taken to Nova Scotia by the British, found living in Canada to be favorable and remained. To this day, a small contingent of Afrodescendants remains in Nova Scotia and thrive in a tightly knit community in this very northern portion of Canada.

These Afrodescendants clearly considered the odds of being on the losing side of a North American war. Yet, they must have concluded that it was a win-win situation to side with the British: Either they would win and be granted freedom in the U.S. or they would be granted freedom outside of the U.S. It was all about freedom, which made their choice a "no brainer."

The American Colonization Society[6]

A major organized effort to return Black Americans to Africa *en masse* by the American Colonization Society (ACS) began in 1817, was at its peak during the 1830s and 1840s, and continued on a less vigorous basis until nearly the turn of the 20th century. The ACS reflected the interests of Afrodescendants who wanted freedom at all cost. At the same time, because the movement was organized and supported in part by the U.S. Government, the movement reflected the racist attitudes of many White Americans who essentially wanted to see Afrodescendants excluded from

---

[6]Alan Yarema's (2006). *The American Colonization Society: An Avenue to Freedom?* University Press of America, Inc. Lanham, MD.

life in the U.S. The latter sentiment was particularly true of White Southerners who wanted to see free southern Blacks removed from the scene so that they could not serve as a reminder to slaves concerning the benefits of freedom.

Over the course of the nearly 80 years that the ACS operated, around 20,000 Black Americans were returned to various locations mainly along Africa's western coast. Many more former slave and free Blacks would have likely returned to African had the cost of returning not been prohibitive. Africa continues to feel the effects of this reverse migration today. As a case in point, Liberia is just beginning to reassemble its nation after a bloody civil war that was sparked mainly by political and economic differences between indigenous Liberians and descendants of free Blacks and slaves from America.

Although the ACS did not yield a mass exodus of Afrodescendants from the U.S., its very existence— whether viewed as a racist or freedom-providing organization—provided an extended dim light for Afrodescendants who desired complete liberation. No question about it, Afrodescendants experienced a liberation as a result of the Emancipation Proclamation. However, for Afrodescendants who desired to live a completely unencumbered life, Africa shone as a light of hope. The ACS provided a means for returning to Africa and enjoying such complete liberation.

53

Paul Cuffee[7]

On December 10, 1815, Paul Cuffee, a free and wealthy Afrodescendant, sailed out of Westport, Massachusetts with 38 passengers. His destination was Sierra Leone where a colony of Afrodescendants already existed. As mentioned above, the colony was founded, in part, by Afrodescendants who had received their freedom as a result of fighting with the British during the American Revolutionary War and the War of 1812.

A free Black with a free Black father and Native American mother, Cuffee became a mariner at an early age. He worked diligently to develop a fleet of vessels and became wealthy transporting goods across the open seas. He came to the realization that emigration provided a real alternative to enjoying limited freedoms in the United States. Before his 1815 voyage, he had traveled to Sierra Leone to explore the possibilities and concluded that life in a colony in that country was an improvement in well-being over residing in the U.S. as a free Black.

Although Cuffee became familiar with the efforts of the American Colonization Society (ACS) later in life, he recognized the racist position of certain factions within the ACS. As discussed above, the latter factions saw emigration back to Africa as a method designed to remove free Blacks from the southern part of the U.S. because they were viewed as a troublesome and constant reminder to Black slaves of the benefits of freedom. Nevertheless, Cuffee recognized the real benefits that were associated with leaving the U.S. and enjoying true liberty and equality.

---

[7]Lamont D. Thomas' (1988) *Paul Cuffee: Black Entrepreneur and Pan-Africanist*, Urbana and Chicago: University of Illinois Press, Chicago, IL.

Cuffee returned to the U.S. after his 1815 voyage. However, he never had an opportunity to return to Sierra Leone. Nevertheless, he spent his remaining years advising Afrodescendants in key cities along the northeastern seaboard of the U.S. to use available resources to plan a permanent transition back to Africa.

Denmark Vessey[8]

It is important, on occasion, to acknowledge unsuccessful attempts. In this case, a slave rebellion was put down that was organized by Denmark Vessey in the Charleston, South Carolina area. We record these events here because the ultimate goal of participants of the rebellion was to escape to Haiti after destroying their slave masters.

According to historian Douglas Egerton, Denmark Vessey was a free black (he purchased his freedom using funds won through a lottery) who resided in Charleston. He was a successful carpenter, and he helped found an African Methodist Episcopal Church in Charleston. Unfortunately, White leadership in Charleston took it upon itself to shut down church operations during 1818 and 1820. For these and other reasons, Vessey is reported as organizing a rebellion that was known to thousands of slave and free Blacks in the Charleston area. The rebellion was to take place on July 14, 1822 (Bastille Day). As mentioned, Whites were to be massacred and Blacks were to escape to Haiti to avoid retaliation. Whites were informed about the rebellion by a couple of slaves who opposed the action. Whites were able to marshal forces and arrest, convict, and execute Vessey and over one hundred of his comrades.

---

[8]Douglas R. Egerton's (2004) *He Shall Go Out Free: The Lives of Denmark Vessey,* 2nd edition, Rowan and Littlefield, Lanham, MD.

Vessey's planned rebellion, although unsuccessful, reflects strong Afrodescendant sentiments concerning departing the U.S. to attain liberty. In other words, if it had been possible to simply sail off to Haiti, then the planned massacre would not have been necessary. As it turned out, such freedom of movement was not possible; hence the bloody plans and the bloody end to Denmark Vessey. Nevertheless, his name and his plan have served as a rallying cry for many Afrodescendants since that fateful day in 1822.

Abraham Lincoln's Chiriqui Plan[9]

President Abraham Lincoln's Chiriqui Plan represents the fifth pre-20th century effort to facilitate Afrodescendants' emigration to distant shores. In this case, President Lincoln advocated that Afrodescendants establish a homeland in an area that is now comprised of Panama, Nicaragua, Honduras, and Costa Rica. Actually, Clarence Lusane provides a thorough account of this plan in his recent work, *The Black History of the White House.*

Lusane makes clear the point that President Lincoln's plan reflected the latter's conviction that Afrodescendants were not equal to Whites and would, therefore, never be treated equally in the U.S. Moreover, Lincoln viewed Black slaves as a key cause of the Civil War. He thought that he could minimize the impact of the war and its aftermath by simply convincing Afrodescendants to head south to Central America.

While certain Afrodescendants backed the Chiriqui Plan, others, including Frederick Douglass, thought the plan a bad idea. The plan certainly did not take shape according

---

[9]Clarence Lusane's (2011), T*he Black History of the White House*, City Lights Books, San Francisco, CA.

to Lincoln's desires. In fact, the plan was altered dramatically, and in April of 1863, some 400 Afrodescendants left the U.S. for an island off the coast of Haiti known as Île á Vache. However, due to poor planning and preparation, 365 of those émigrés who did not die on the island returned to the U.S. after about a year.

The Chiriqui Plan was unsuccessful for a variety of reasons; however, a key reason was that wide-spread support was not forthcoming from Afrodescendant leadership. It could be that at this stage of the Civil War, Afrodescendants were of the mind that freedom could be achieved. The reality is that Reconstruction did produce sizeable improvements to Afrodescendant participation in American democracy and to the quality of life for former slaves. But, as we all know, this was a relatively short-lived outcome.

20th Century Nation Formation Efforts

Marcus Garvey[10]

Having already established the Universal Negro Improvement Association (UNIA) and African Communities (Imperial) League in Jamaica, Marcus Garvey arrived in the U.S. in 1916 and established a division of the UNIA in 1917. Garvey was able to fill a hole left by the absence of strong Black leadership for the average Afrodescendant in the U.S., and to stimulate a strong interest in Black Nationalism.

The UNIA developed a variety of businesses, including the Black Star Lines shipping company, which was designed to

---

[10]Robert A. Hill's (Editor) (1987), *Marcus Garvey Life & Lessons*, University of California Press, Los Angeles, CA.

not only ship Black-produced products but to also help transport Afrodescendants back to Africa. Garvey used his businesses and popularity to urge the development of an African territory to which Afrodescendants could emigrate. In this regard, his focus was on Liberia, but he encountered opposition from business interests that were already established in that nation.

Although Garvey undoubtedly incited a high level of interest in Black Nationalism or Pan Africanism through his UNIA efforts, there is no evidence that the UNIA was responsible directly for relocating large numbers of Afrodescendants from the Americas back to Africa. However, there is abundant evidence that down through the course of history Marcus Garvey was instrumental in linking Africa and the New World. Probably the most outstanding example of the Garvey factor can be seen in the actions taken by Kwame Nkrumah, the President of Ghana at independence (1957), who adopted a flag for his country, which reflects UNIA colors (red, black, and green) and a black star. Nkrumah also named Ghana's shipping company the Black Star Lines. In the U.S., Garvey's influence and power can be observed in the work of those that were to follow; especially the work of the Honorable Elijah Muhammad (see below) and one of the latter's most ardent followers, Malcolm X, whose parents met at a UNIA convention.

The record shows that Garvey was indicted on trumped up mail fraud charges by the forerunner of today's Federal Bureau of Investigation. He was jailed in 1925 in connection with a five-year sentence. In 1927, President Calvin Coolidge commuted his sentence, and he was deported back to Jamaica. Nevertheless, Garvey's very strong Black Nationalism movement planted seeds that continue to produce organizational efforts today that are designed to motivate Afrodescendants to seriously consider pulling up their roots and returning to Africa.

Elijah Muhammad[11]

Building on knowledge that he received from Master Fard Muhammad, the Honorable Elijah Muhammad built an expansive religious and business empire from the 1930s to the mid-1970s. Characterizing himself as "The Messenger," his task was to awaken Afrodescendants in the U.S., clean them up (because "they were fit for no one"), and prepare them to rejoin "their own"—presumably the African or Asiatic Black man.

It is not unexpected that the Honorable Elijah Muhammad taught his followers to entertain going back to Africa because he was familiar with the Marcus Garvey Movement. Yet, if one reads the former's writings carefully, there appears to be some ambiguity about his plans for his people. There are endless references in the Honorable Elijah Muhammad's writings to obtaining some of this "good earth" to use in production. On certain occasions, he discusses the failure of American Whites to set aside a portion of the country for Afrodescendants to use as their own. On the other hand, especially during the last decade or so of his life, he teaches explicitly of America's downfall. Consequently, he states quite clearly, in spots, that Afrodescendants should quit America.

This ambiguity can be rationalized by interpreting the Honorable Elijah Muhammad's writings to mean that Afrodescendants should quit America for an area that would be set aside strictly for Blacks that would be

---

[11]Elijah Muhammad's (1965), *Message to the Blackman in America,* Secretarius MEMPS Ministries, Phoenix, AZ.

considered outside of America. An explicit statement to this effect can be found in his most famous work, *Message to the Blackman in America*, where he says:

> "So, therefore, we should look forward and try to get the government to agree to let us go somewhere by ourselves and build a nation of our own and on some of this land that we helped get." (p. 312)

Clearly, this is a unique arrangement where Afrodescendants are expected to go out but within. It is a very logical approach to the problem due to the prohibitive costs that are associated with trying to move millions of Afrodescendants across the Atlantic Ocean back to Africa. Importantly, it satisfies the desires of many Afrodescendants who feel that the U.S. owes them and their ancestors' payment for the lives and years of toil and struggle involved in helping build the nation at home and abroad. In essence, the Honorable Elijah Muhammad placed complete liberty for Afrodescendants at our fingertips—if only the U.S. Government can be convinced.

Three Independent Living Cases

Wilmington, North Carolina[12]

The November 10, 1898 race riot in Wilmington, North Carolina represents probably the most prototypical case of racism where Whites refused to recognize the economic success of Afrodescendants. White racists banned together and violently murdered and injured Afrodescendants in

---

[12]LeRae S. Umfleet's (2009) *A Day of Blood: The 1898 Wilmington Race Riot*, North Carolina Office of Archives and History and the African American Heritage Commission, Raleigh, NC.

order to send a forceful message that that success would not be tolerated.

By the late 1890s, Wilmington had become a Mecca for Afrodescendants in North Carolina. It boasted a large population of skilled artisans (carpenters, masons, mechanics), stevedores who operated Wilmington's important marine port, and professionals in medicine, law, education, and the clergy. Afrodescendant homeownership was said to be higher in Wilmington than in any other part of the nation, in part because Afrodescendants pooled their resources and formed a financial institution to supply mortgages to home buyers. Most importantly, Blacks occupied key elected and appointed positions in a Republican Party controlled government.

White Democrats could not stomach such success and plotted to remove Republicans, especially Black Republicans from power. Using a "White Declaration of Independence" as the framework for their action, which was motivated by an editorial in a local Afrodescendant newspaper, White Democrat vigilantes burned Afrodescendant-owned structures and killed and injured an untold number of Blacks. One report places the death toll at as many as 250 Afrodescendants.

In conjunction with the riot, White Democrats forced a change in Wilmington's government, which saw their rise to power. Since that fateful day, Afrodescendants have not been able to realize the same power status in the city— economically or politically.

These events highlight the behavior of racist Whites who refused to permit Afrodescendants to forge their way into the mainstream of American society by relying on an intense work ethic and by using the ballot. The independent and successful Afrodescendant population in Wilmington had integrated itself well into key economic and political positions prior to the riots. They threatened to achieve equality with, and possibly surpass, Whites on all fronts given sufficient opportunities and time. This was something that Whites simply refused to permit.

Tulsa, Oklahoma[13]

On May 31, 1921, Afrodescendants from the Greenwood District of Tulsa (the "Black Wall Street"), gathered at the courthouse to protest the expected lynching of Richard Rowland, who had been charged with sexually assaulting a White female—charges that were dropped after the riot. Whites had also gathered at the court house. A shot was fired, Afrodescendants retreated to the Greenwood area, and Whites pursued them.

The riot that ensued lasted until the next day. Whites burned and looted up to 40 blocks of the Greenwood section of Tulsa, to include homes (over 1,200), businesses, schools, a hospital, a library, and churches. It is reported that even an airplane was used as part of the Whites' attack on Greenwood. Tulsa police officials helped fuel the riot by deputizing White males and raiding gun shops to arm them. When it was over, very little remained of Greenwood, and up to 300 Afrodescendants were dead.

Greenwood had been developed by Afrodescendants who had benefitted significantly from an oil boom. The community contained a sizeable population that had well-developed businesses and high-quality institutions. Certain

---

[13]Danney Goble's (2000), *Final Report of the Commission to Study the Tulsa Race Riot of 1921,* Commission to Study the Tulsa Race Riot of 1921, Tulsa, OK. Retrieved July 12, 2011; http://www.tulsareparations.org/FinalReport.htm .

members of the commission that was organized to study the riot in 2000 concluded that Whites, including members of the Ku Klux Klan, conspired to bring Greenwood down—presumably because of their jealousy and anger against successful Afrodescendants. Unfortunately, the commission did not divulge in its final report an estimate of the value of the damage and destruction that occurred during the riot.

Although great effort has gone into resurrecting the historical details of the Tulsa Race Riot, the Oklahoma Legislature and U.S. courts have ruled that no reparations are to be paid for the victims of the riot—several of whom are alive and still reside in Tulsa today.

Rosewood, Florida[14]

Reparations have been paid to survivors of the 1923 Rosewood, Florida Race Riot. Rosewood was a settlement in central Florida that had a population of over 300. A couple of dominant Afrodescendant families (the Goins and the Carriers) operated turpentine and logging businesses, respectively, in and around Rosewood and helped the community flourish economically. Many of the Afrodescendant families in the community were wealthy enough to have pianos and organs in their homes—signs of middle-class affluence. The settlement included a couple of churches, a school, and a few business establishments. The Afrodescendants in this community lived virtually independently.

---

[14] Maxine Jones, Larry Rivers, David Colburn, R. Tom Dye, and William Rogers, (1993), *Documented History of the Incident Which Occurred At Rosewood, Florida in January 1923*, Tallahassee, FL. Retrieved July 12, 2011 ; http://www.displaysforschools.com/rosewoodrp.html#top.

On January 1, 1923, a Ms. Fannie Taylor, who lived near Rosewood, claimed that she was attacked by an Afrodescendant male. After word spread about this incident, individual attacks on Afrodescendant males began. By January 4th, a group of Whites bent on revenge for Taylor visited Rosewood and attacked a home where several Afrodescendants were held up. During a shooting standoff, at least two Whites and six Afrodescendants died. Despite the loss of life, the Afrodescendants in the home did not surrender.

This standoff involving Afrodescendants defending themselves against attacks by Whites fueled even more anger on the part of Whites. On January 5th, White vigilantes came to Rosewood and burned homes and other structures to the ground. Afrodescendants who were lucky enough to escape the individual and group attacks and the burning, hid in nearby swamps, were protected by Whites who opposed the attacks, or made their way by train and other means to nearby towns and cities, such as Gainesville.

The story of Rosewood was mum for decades until the 1980s when survivors resurrected the history. After suing for reparations because law enforcement officials failed to protect the citizens of Rosewood, the State of Florida paid reparations to survivors.

Importantly, exploration of the Rosewood Massacre ushered up a survivor who contended that the Taylor story included false claims. Apparently, Taylor had a White lover who assaulted her on that fateful January 1, 1923 day. Sadly, the chain of events in Rosewood resulted in the deaths of 25 or more Afrodescendants. Again, Whites found it difficult to respect the success of an Afrodescendant community, and allowed very flimsy evidence to produce a race riot. Nevertheless, the residents of Rosewood will always be remembered for their independence, their self-defense efforts, and their resourcefulness, which helped many of them to survive the onslaught of White racists.

Conclusion

If conditions are not expected to improve substantially for Afrodescendants in the U.S. over the next 40 years, then it may be worthwhile to consider shaking up the status quo. One option is to undertake a nation formation effort. This chapter answers the question, "what is the history of nation formation and independent living efforts in the U.S. for Afrodescendants?" The literature recounts five notable pre-20th century nation formation cases, and three important independent living cases. As a bonus, we also discussed two personality driven 20th century efforts that focused on an exodus for Afrodescendants.

We found a range of outcomes. In certain cases, Afrodescendants purposely sought to exit the U.S. in a search for liberty. In other cases, White Americans attempted to organize and direct efforts to expel Afrodescendant from the U.S. Whatever the circumstances, Afrodescendants were not always willing partners. Often there was forceful opposition to the idea of leaving the U.S.

We also found that when Afrodescendants were able to forge economic and/or political successes by exercising their right to independent development, Whites inevitably found this success to be unacceptable. Wilmington, Tulsa, and Rosewood are emblematic of White fears that Afrodescendants, when permitted the freedom to develop properly, may surpass their White counterparts. In the

22

mind of White America, this is a condition that must not be permitted.

Today, we live in the 21st century and we have 400 years of experience in America. There is no question that certain Afrodescendants are experiencing a very high quality of life today. To be frank, that has always been the case. The case of Paul Cuffee is a prime example of how certain Afrodescendants have enjoyed wealth in the U.S. from the very outset. However, for the majority of Afrodescendants, the story has been dismal. Whether we refer to cotton-picking slaves in Mississippi, sharecroppers in Arkansas, meat packers in slaughter houses, low-level factory workers in the nation's urban centers, or the 25%-to-40% of Afrodescendant males who are unemployed (once discouraged workers are counted) during today's aftermath of the great recession, conditions are not so favorable. Would we not be wise to consider a different path than the path of patience—waiting for liberty and equality to evolve?

About one thing we can be certain: If we do not act to change circumstances, then it is unlikely that circumstances will change. In addition, if the people of Southern Sudan can venture to found a new nation with their knowledges, skills, abilities, and expertise, then how much more successful could Afrodescendants perform in founding our own new nation?

The entire purpose of this monograph, *53*, is to show that if we abide in the status quo, then conditions will not improve. Therefore, Afrodescendants have a choice to change the status quo. We have a history of thoughts of, and actions toward, exodus. To date, we do not have a perfect exodus story. However, our history mirrors perfectly the pre-Exodus Biblical story. What we do not know is the number of pre-Moses period unrecorded efforts by the Hebrews to exodus Egypt? Maybe a confluence of events is forming, which may lead us down to the Red Sea (a sea of red ink being faced by U.S. Governments at all levels). We are hopeful that we will have the courage to cross to a new land that bears a promise of liberty and equality-because we will be with our own.

Chapter 3.—Black America: 2010-2050 in *53*

In this chapter, our goal is to develop reasonable statistical forecasts that indicate the likely state of Black American affairs at mid-21st-century. As highlighted in the introductory chapter, we will use this chapter to develop these forecasts using the "53" paradigm. Just to reiterate, the seven key variables for which forecasts will be presented include: Population, employment, income, entrepreneurship, educational attainment, criminal justice, and health.

We begin our effort to forecast each variable with a replica of Figure 2 (see Chapter 1), which is modified specifically for the series under consideration. In the figure we interpret how the three classes of Black Americans are likely to impact the five action scenarios. To accomplish this, we apply appropriate weighted adjustments to our starting point, status quo, and conservative trend forecast, which fits the "Do Nothing" action scenario. We follow up the figure with text that explains how the status quo forecast is constructed, and we provide insights concerning important information that informs our adjustments of the status quo forecasts within the context of the "53" paradigm.

At the chapter's conclusion we will use these forecasts to identify what appears to be statistically favorable courses of action for Black Americans based on the five action scenarios that we believe could be operational over the next 40 years. We then discuss the likelihood that the favorable path indicated by the forecasts will be adopted by Black Americans.

Population

Population is the logical variable to begin with in this analysis because it helps determine how many Blacks will be present in the future. As a starting point, we constructed the "Do Nothing" series by averaging two series. The first was an extrapolation of the 2010 census population value for Black or African Americans (alone) using the average annual rate of population growth (1.39%) for Blacks during 1910-2010.[15] The second was constructed beginning with the 2010 population, subtracting from each subsequent year the average Black mortality rate (1,038.888 per 100,000 population) during 2003-05 and adding the crude Black birth rate (15.966 per 1,000 population) during 2003-05 plus 90,000 (a judgmental estimate) to account for Black immigration.[16]

Do Nothing	This is the status quo forecast.
Accelerate Integration	Upper-middle and upper-class population accelerates intermarriage with other ethnic groups (weighted effect).
Resegregate	All three classes of Blacks constrain the rate at which intermarrying occurs (weighted effect).
Diaspora	Upper-middle class population emigrates abroad (weighted effect).
Nation Formation	Lower-middle and lower class population relocates outside of the U.S. in 2050 guided by a small *intelligencia* of upper middle-income Blacks (weighted effect).

Figure 3.—Population in the "53" Paradigm

---

[15] See the Censuses of Population at www.census.gov.
[16] The data on death rates and crude birth rates were from the National Center for Health Statistics (2009), *Health, United States, 2008 With Chartbook*, Hyattsville, MD (pp. 204 and 162, respectively).

Figure 3 presents assumptions for adjustments to the status quo ("Do Nothing") series in the context of the "53" paradigm. In the case of "Accelerate Integration," we assume that upper and upper-middle-class Blacks will accelerate the rate at which Afrodescendants intermarry with other ethnic groups, producing mixed offspring, and thereby lowering the Black population. The 2000 census showed that the ratio of Blacks of multiple races to Black alone was over 5% percent. For 2010, that ratio had grown to nearly 8%. We developed the "Accelerate Integration" population series by subtracting from the normal growth rate (i.e., the growth rate of the "Do Nothing" series) of the Black alone population about 8% of newly born Blacks each year (based on the aforementioned 2003-2005 crude birth rate), plus we accelerated the rate at which that subtraction occurred by about 4.6% each year based on the growth rate at which the ratio of multiple race Blacks to Black alone grew during the period 2000 to 2010.

For "Resegregation," we invert the calculation used for "Accelerate Integration" by simply adding back into the normal growth rate of the Black alone population the approximately 8% of the newly born Black alone population that was previously contributing to the growth in the number of Blacks with multiple races.

For "Diaspora," we judgmentally assume that a very small percentage (0.5%) of the upper-middle class (which comprises about 25% of the total Black population) emigrate to other countries each year. On one hand, certain components of the upper-class population consider themselves doing well in the U.S. and, therefore, have no incentive to emigrate. On the other hand, some wealthy Blacks see that they can fare better outside of the U.S.

For the "Nation Formation" series, we model this event as a 40-year planning process that culminates in the shifting of 10% of the population (mainly lower and lower-middle-class) to a location outside of the U.S. as we know it today to establish an independent nation state. We anticipate that they will be led by a small *intelligencia*, which comes from the upper and upper-middle class. We assume that the new Black nation state begins its history in 2050.

Table 1 provides our five sets of decennial forecasts for the Black population from 2010 to 2050.

Table 1.—Black Population Forecasts: 2010-2050
(millions)

Action Scenario	2010	2020	2030	2040	2050
Do Nothing	38.9	43.4	48.3	53.9	60.1
Accelerate Integration	38.9	42.8	47.1	51.8	57.0
Resegregate	38.9	43.9	49.6	55.9	63.2
Diaspora	38.9	42.8	47.2	51.9	57.2
Nation Formation	38.9	42.4	48.3	53.9	54.1

It is worth mentioning that the U.S. Census Bureau has projected the Black population to stand at 62 million by 2050; therefore, our status quo ("Do Nothing") estimate is conservative.[17] Notably, the Census Bureau estimate was prepared during the 1990s. An Internet Web site entitled *Black Demographics* places the 2050 Black population in the 56.9 million to 65.7 million range; a mid-point for the latter would hit the Census Bureau's 62 million mark.[18]

53

---

[17] See "Population Profile of the United States" at http://www.census.gov/population/www/pop-profile/natproj.html.
[18] See "Future Black Population" at http://www.blackdemographics.com/.

Employment

Our analysis of employment in the "53" paradigm is captured in Figure 4.

Do Nothing	This is the status quo forecast
Accelerate Integration	Upper-middle and upper-class population accelerates intermarriage with other ethnic groups (weighted effect); mixed-race blacks capture employment formerly available to Blacks.
Resegregate	All three classes of Blacks constrain the rate at which intermarrying occurs (weighted effect); absence of mixed-race Blacks increases growth in employment for the former.
Diaspora	Upper-middle class population emigrate abroad (weighted effect); the growth rate of Black employment decelerates.
Nation Formation	The lower-middle and lower class population relocates outside of the U.S. in 2050 guided by a small *intelligencia* of upper-middle class Blacks (weighted effect); Black employment declines in 2050.

Figure 4.—Employment in the "53" Paradigm

We prepared employment estimates beginning with the previously-described population estimates for the aforementioned five categories. Using data from the Bureau of Labor Statistics (BLS) Current Population Survey (CPS) we derived the Black civilian non-institutional population (CNIP) above the age of 16 using the 2009 CNIP-to total population ratio.[19] To account for

---

[19] Historical CPS CNIP data on Black employment are available at www.bls.gov.

the aging nature of the Black American population, we grew the 2009 CNIP-to total population ratio (.7374) by about 0.2% throughout the forecast period, which was the rate at which the ratio had grown between 1980 and 2009. We then derived labor force and employment estimates by applying average labor force- and employment-to-CNIP ratios that were computed from CPS data for the period 1972-2009. The average labor force-to-CNIP was 0.629 and the average employment-to-labor force ratio was 0.878, implying an average unemployment rate of 12.2%. These ratios were not adjusted during the forecast period because they are volatile and their average historical values are rational values to adopt for the forecast. The employment estimates appear in Table 2.

Table 2.—Black Employment Forecasts: 2010-2050 (millions)

Action Scenario	2010	2020	2030	2040	2050
Do Nothing	15.0	18.1	20.6	23.5	26.8
Accelerate Integration	15.0	17.8	20.1	22.6	25.4
Resegregate	15.0	18.3	21.1	24.4	28.2
Diaspora	15.0	17.8	20.1	22.6	25.5
Nation Formation	15.0	18.1	20.6	23.5	24.1

Readers are cautioned to keep in mind that each of the five scenarios in the "53" paradigm is considered to be mutually exclusive in this context. Such a perspective aids with the interpretation and analysis of the data that are presented in Table 2.

Income

A key factor for income growth in the "53" paradigm is the role of mixed-raced (light-skinned) Blacks who are assumed to appear under the "Accelerate Integration" scenario. For purposes of this analysis, we follow the scholarship of Goldsmith, Hamilton, and Darity (2007) who conclude that, in general, light-skinned Blacks garner about a 10% higher level of compensation when compared with other Blacks.[20] We invite readers to consult the three co-authors' work to obtain a full understanding of this conclusion, but essentially, the idea is that employers have a preference for light-skinned Blacks over medium- and dark-skinned Blacks. We build on this research by assuming that mixed-race Blacks will have the same phenotypical characteristics of light-skinned Blacks, and will, therefore, receive a higher level of compensation, when compared to Blacks. Consequently, increases or decreases in the population of mixed-race Blacks is expected to place downward or upward pressure, respectively, on the incomes that Blacks receive.

Given the foregoing as context, consider Figure 5.

Do Nothing	This is the status quo forecast
Accelerate Integration	Upper-middle and upper-class population accelerates intermarriage with other ethnic groups (weighted effect); mixed-race Blacks with light skin capture higher levels of income and depress Black alone income.
Resegregate	All three classes of Blacks constrain the rate at which intermarrying occurs; the absence of mixed-race Blacks places upward pressure on Black income.
Diaspora	Upper-middle class population emigrate abroad (weighted effect); a reduced supply of Black labor places upward pressure on income

[20]See Arthur Goldsmith, Darrick Hamilton, and William Darity (2007), "From Dark to Light: Skin Color and Wages Among African-Americans." *Journal of Human Resources*: Vol. 42, No. 4; pp 701-38.

Nation Formation	Lower-middle and lower class population relocates outside of the U.S. in 2050, guided by a small *intelligencia* from among upper-middle class Blacks (weighted effect); a 10% decline in the Black population in 2050 causes a concomitant 10% increase in Black income.

Figure 5.—Income in the "53" Paradigm

The income estimates are from the Census Bureau and represent mean household income.[21] The following are details of how the five income series were generated. Given the powerful economic developments that have occurred in the global economy over the past decade, which are expected to be long-lasting, we constructed the "Do Nothing" series by growing income over the forecast period at a 1.81% rate—the rate of income growth over the past nine years. The "Accelerate Integration" series was derived by subtracting 10% of the growth in the "Do Nothing" series, and growing that deduction by the rate at which mixed-race Blacks are expected to enter the population. Again, this is based on the assumption that mixed-race Blacks will garner higher income (10%) and, thereby, suppress Blacks' income. For the "Resegregate series," we invert the calculation for the "Accelerate Integration" series, and increase the growth in the "Do Nothing" series by 10%. For the "Diaspora" series, we increase the "Do Nothing" series' growth rate by the growth in the number of Black émigrés. For the "Nation Formation" series, in 2050, we increase Black income by 10% to account for the upward pressure on compensation that will result when 10% of the Black population exits to

---

[21] Census Bureau income statistics are available at http://www.census.gov/hhes/www/income/data/historical/household/index.html.

form a nation. The income forecasts for 2010-2050 appear
in Table 3.

Table 3.—Black Income Forecasts: 2010-2050
($'s Thousands)

Action Scenario	2010	2020	2030	2040	2050
Do Nothing	46.9	56.1	67.1	80.3	96.1
Accelerate Integration	46.9	55.0	64.6	75.9	89.2
Resegregate	46.9	57.2	69.7	84.9	103.4
Diaspora	46.9	56.2	67.4	81.1	97.8
Nation Formation	46.9	56.1	67.1	80.3	105.7

Clearly, the most favorable outcomes, income wise,
involves the "Nation Formation" and "Resegregation"
scenarios—both scenarios may be viewed by many Black
Americans today as suboptimal outcomes. In the former
case, we would have to lose 10% of the Black population to
engender a substantial rise in income in 2050. In the latter
case, Black Americans would have to resegregate
themselves and constrain the production of mixed-race
(light-skinned) Blacks in order to capture a higher level of
income over the period, which would normally be reserved
for light-skinned Blacks.

Entrepreneurship

Entrepreneurship has at least two important dimensions:
(1) The number of firms; and (2) the number of employees.
We constrain ourselves here to forecasting the number of
Black firms that will exist during 2010-2050. In 1969, the
Census Bureau performed its first comprehensive
assessment of Black-owned businesses. Its second such
assessment was conducted in 1972, and the Census Bureau
has performed these assessments in each subsequent five-
year interval in accordance with required quinquennial
censuses. We use these data to capture trends that can be

33

adopted for the future. Figure 6 conveys our assumptions about entrepreneurial growth within the "53" paradigm.

.

Do Nothing	This is the status quo forecast
Accelerate Integration	Upper-middle and upper-class population accelerates intermarriage with other ethnic groups (weighted effect); fewer Blacks create reduced demand for Black firms.
Resegregate	All three classes of Blacks constrain the rate at which intermarrying occurs (weighted effect); increased Black population increases the demand for Black firms.
Diaspora	Upper-middle class population emigrating abroad (weighted effect); a reduced Black population reduces the demand for Black firms.
Nation Formation	Lower-middle and lower class population relocates outside of the U.S. in 2050 guided by a small *intelligencia* of upper-middle class Blacks (weighted effect); a reduced Black population reduces the demand for Black firms, plus Black businesses emigrate as part of "Nation Formation."

Figure 6.—Entrepreneurship in the "53" Paradigm

We develop the "Do Nothing" forecast by growing the 2007 number of Black firms by the average annual growth rate identified in the Census Bureau data over the 1969-2002 period.[22] The growth in Black businesses over the 2002-2007 period was at a just under 10% rate—a rate that is unsustainable. Therefore, we adopt a more reasonable

---

[22] The Census Bureau data on Black-owned businesses is at http://www.census.gov/econ/sbo/ (Survey of Business Ownership). We adopt one-half of the 1969-2007 growth rate to account for attrition. It is common knowledge that about one-half of small businesses fail within five years.

rate of growth for Black business of about 4.1%, which prevailed over the 1969-2002 period. For the "Accelerate Integration" forecast, we reduce the growth in Black firms implied by the "Do Nothing" series by the growth in the mixed-race Blacks (i.e., the difference in the "Do Nothing" and "Accelerate Integration" population series). For "Resegregation," we invert the "Accelerate Integration" series and grow the number of Black firms by the rate at which mixed-race Blacks would be curtailed and the number of "Black alone" would expand through resegregation. For the "Diaspora" series, we reduce the growth in Black firms implied by the "Do Nothing" series by the rate at which Blacks emigrate. For the "Nation Formation" series, in 2050, we reduce the number of Black firms by computing per capita Black firms under the "Do Nothing" scenario and determining the number of firms that would be lost by a 10% exit of the Black population.

Table 4 provides forecasts of the number of Black firms that we expect to be in existence during 2010-2050.

Table 4.—Black Entrepreneurship Forecasts: 2010-2050
(Thousands of firms)

Action Scenario	2010	2020	2030	2040	2050
Do Nothing	2166	3225	4801	7149	10644
Accelerate Integration	2166	3216	4750	6983	10213
Resegregate	2166	3234	4853	7319	11092
Diaspora	2166	3216	4753	6992	10237
Nation Formation	2166	3225	4801	7149	9580

Even if Black Americans do not maintain such a rapid pace of entrepreneurialism and we overstate somewhat the number of Black firms in existence by 2050, we can still use Table 4 to envision the relative impacts of the five action scenarios, which can help us make decisions about the "best" course of action for Black Americans.

Average Years of Schooling

We adopt "Average Years of Schooling" (AYS) for the Black population over the age of 18 to represent the level of education or academic achievement. This is an important measure for determining prospects for Black employment, income, development, and overall well-being. Annual statistics on years of education completed are collected through the Census Bureau's Current Population Survey (CPS). These data are tabulated by the National Center for Education Statistics, and published in the *Digest of Education Statistics*.[23] We developed AYS annual values by applying population shares to 11 categories of education completion, which were associated with specific years of schooling: Less than 7 years (5); 7-8 years (7.5); 1-3 years of high school (10); 4 years of high school (11); completed high school (12); some college (13); Associates Degree (14); Bachelor's Degree (16); Master's Degree (18); Professional Degree (19); and Doctorate Degree (20)—years of schooling are in parenthesis.

As with the income variable, we assume that light-skinned/mixed-race Blacks reflect an elevated rate of educational attainment over that of the population that is "Black alone." This assumption is based primarily on research conducted by Margaret L. Hunter (1999), who concludes that skin tone is correlated, in a significant way, with educational attainment—the lighter the skin, the more education attained.[24] Although more recent studies (namely Gullickson (2003) and Loury (2009)) contend that skin tone is less of a factor in determining educational

---

[23] Data on years of schooling completed are published in Table 9 of the *Digest of Education Statistics*; http://nces.ed.gov/programs/digest/.
[24] See Margaret Hunter's article, "Colorstruck: Skin Color Stratification in the Lives of African American Women," *Sociological Inquiry*: Vol. 68, No. 4: 517-35.

attainment for more recent, younger cohorts of Blacks, they continue to find evidence that skin tone is a factor in determining outcomes in some aspects of Black Americans' lives.[25]

Figure 7 reflects our interpretation of the AYS variable in the "53" paradigm.

Do Nothing	This is the status quo forecast
Accelerate Integration	Upper-middle and upper-class population accelerates intermarriage with other ethnic groups (weighted effect); Blacks (alone) have a reduced rate of educational attainment.
Resegregate	All three classes of Blacks constrain the rate at which intermarrying occurs (weighted effect); while more in number, resegregated Blacks (alone) have an unchanged ("Do Nothing") rate of educational attainment.
Diaspora	Upper-middle class population emigrate abroad (weighted effect); Blacks (alone) are fewer in number and have reduced educational attainment.

---

[25] See Aaron Gullickson's article, "The Significance of Color Declines: a Re-analysis of Skin Tone Effects in the National Survey of Black Americans," which is a conference paper that was delivered to the American Sociological Association in 2003. Also see Linda Loury's article, "Am I Still Too Black for You? Schooling and Secular Change in Skin Tone Effects," *Economics of Education Review*: Vol. 28, No. 4; 428-33.

Nation Formation	Lower-middle and lower class population relocates outside of the U.S. in 2050 guided by a small *intelligencia* of upper-middle class Blacks (weighted effect); the loss of lower echelon Blacks causes the Average Years of Schooling to rise for those that remain.

Figure 7.—Average Years of Schooling in the "53" paradigm

We estimate the "Do Nothing Series" by growing the 2010 AYS (12.79 years) by the average annual increase that has been exhibited by Blacks during 1994-2010 (.004 years). The "Accelerate Integration" series is estimated by assuming that the loss of mixed-race (light-skinned) Blacks reduces the AYS by an annual percentage that is equal to the number of the mixed-race population as a percentage of "Do Nothing" population. We adopt an identical annual pattern of AYS for the "Resegregate" series as for the "Do Nothing" series because Black (alone) are added to the population, but do not affect the rate of educational attainment. For the "Diaspora" series, we reduce AYS that is reflected in the "Do Nothing" series by the percentage of upper-echelon Black population that is assumed to depart the U.S.—i.e., the percentage of the "Diaspora" to the "Do Nothing" population. For the "Nation Formation" series we boost the "Do Nothing" Average Years of Schooling in 2050 by 10% to reflect a loss mainly of Blacks with lower educational attainment, which permits the AYS to rise for the Blacks that remain. Table 5 presents the AYS forecasts.

53

Table 5.—Average Years of Schooling Forecasts:
2010-2050

Action Scenario	2010	2020	2030	2040	2050
Do Nothing	12.79	13.30	13.83	14.83	14.96
Accelerate Integration	12.79	13.29	13.81	14.35	14.89
Resegregate	12.79	13.30	13.83	14.83	14.96
Diaspora	12.79	13.29	13.81	14.35	14.90
Nation Formation	12.79	13.30	13.83	14.83	16.45

Table 5 reveals that, over the period 2010-2050, the average Afrodescendant over the age of 18 moves from possessing a high school diploma to having more education than that required to possess an Associate's degree. In the case of "Nation Formation," the Blacks that are left behind are expected to have, on average, a Bachelor's Degree.

Incarceration

In 2009, 841,000 Black American males and 64,800 females were estimated to be incarcerated in Federal, State, and local prisons and jails according to the U.S. Department of Justice; 5,082 per 100,000 population. Even the temporary loss of Blacks to incarceration has an impact on all of the previously discussed aspects of Black American life. Although we do not seek to analyze whether Black American sentencing has increased over time or is increasing, we do estimate how the number of Blacks who are incarcerated is expected to unfold over the next 40 years.

Our analysis focuses on the "number incarcerated," and consideration of this variable is undertaken in a "53" paradigm in Figure 8 below.

Do Nothing	This is the status quo forecast
Accelerate Integration	Upper-middle and upper-class population accelerates intermarriage with other ethnic groups (weighted effect); the Black (alone) incarceration rate is not affected by the increase in mixed-race Blacks.
Resegregate	All three classes of Blacks constrain the rate at which intermarrying occurs (weighted effect); given increases in number, resegregated Blacks (alone) experience a slightly higher (1%) rate of incarceration.
Diaspora	Upper-middle class population emigrate abroad (weighted effect); Blacks (alone) are fewer in number but this has no affect on the incarceration rate.
Nation Formation	Lower-middle and lower class population relocates outside of the U.S. in 2050 guided by a small *intelligencia* of upper-middle class Blacks (weighted effect); the loss of lower echelon Blacks has no affect on the incarceration rate of Blacks that remain in 2050.

Figure 8.—Incarceration in the "53" paradigm

From Figure 8 we see that the rate of incarceration per 100,000 of population is expected to hold steady at the average 2000-2009 rate over the period 2010-2050; however, level changes are affected as the population varies for our five scenarios. The data for our analysis come from the U.S. Department of Justice (DOJ), Bureau of Justice Statistics annual publication entitled, *Prison Inmates at Midyear*.[26]

---

[26] The publications are obtainable from the following Internet Web page: http://www.bjs.gov/index.cfm?ty=pbse&sid=38 .

The 2009 edition of *Prison Inmates at Midyear* shows that from 2000-2009, the average number of Black male and female prisoners held per 100,000 averaged 5,136. While this value appears to be very high, it compares favorably with an average of 5,226. Black male and female prisoners per 100,000 population during 1984-1994. In fact, it is quite clear that there was a rapid increase in the rate at which Blacks were incarcerated during the mid-1980s to mid-1990s decade; the rate grew from 3,475 per 100,000 in 1984 to 7,188 per 100,000 in 1994. By 2000, the incarceration rate was down to 5,157 per 100,000.

We prepare forecasts for the analysis by extrapolating the 2009 estimate of the Black prison population using the 5,136 per 100,000 and the population levels that were developed under the "Population" section of this chapter. As a special case—i.e., for the "Resegregation" scenario— we augment the aforementioned extrapolator by increasing it by 1% to account for an increased incarceration rate that would be expected if the Black (alone) population adopted a resegregation strategy.

Table 6 reflects the expected levels of incarceration during 2010-2050 under our five scenarios.

Table 6.—Black Incarceration: 2010-2050[27]
(Thousands)

Action Scenario	2010	2020	2030	2040	2050
Do Nothing	906	1,009	1,125	1,254	1,398
Accelerate Integration	906	996	1,096	1,205	1,327
Resegregate	906	1,129	1,407	1,755	2,188
Diaspora	906	997	1,097	1,208	1,330
Nation Formation	906	1,009	1,125	1,254	1,258

Table 6 highlights that the best end-game is derived from the "Nation Formation" scenario—assuming that certain Black Americans who would be incarcerated find their way into the group that exits the U.S. in 2050. Otherwise, the "Accelerate Integration" and "Diaspora" scenarios prove to be beneficial in limiting the level of Black American incarceration. Given augmented (1%) incarceration rates in the case of "Resegregation," the latter case provides the most unfavorable outcome. However, it stands to reason that, if incarceration is a racialized outcome in the U.S., then the nation would increase its incarceration of Blacks when the Black population expands at an accelerated rate.

Despite our use of long-term averaging to develop trend incarceration estimates out to 2050, some might argue that Federal, state, and local governments' current fiscal condition will force a reduction in incarceration rates. Besides, as discussed above, incarceration rates have been declining slightly. Although we comprehend the logic of these analyses, the reality is that economic circumstances are cyclical. Therefore, the seemingly large Federal budget deficits of the 1980s and 1990s were transformed into an over $200 billion fiscal surplus by 2000. Hence, it may very well be reasonable to conclude that adoption of long-

---

[27]The 2010 values are estimated. Bureau of Justice Statistics data for 2010 were not available at the time of publication.

term trend estimates to project incarceration levels out to 2050 is the correct approach with which to adhere.

Life Expectancy

Randall (2006) has written a very enthralling book entitled, *Dying While Black*.[28] Randall sets as a standard for evaluating Black American health in the U.S. multiple variables. Three of the most important variables are life expectancy, infant mortality, and low birth weight babies. We have selected life expectancy for our analysis, and we perform a two-part analysis: Male versus female life expectancy.

Figure 9 reflects our expectations concerning life expectancy for Black males and females in the "53" paradigm

Do Nothing	This is the status quo forecast
Accelerate Integration	Upper-middle and upper-class population accelerates intermarriage with other ethnic groups (weighted effect); Blacks (alone) who have traditionally received poorer quality healthcare will experience a slower pace of life expectancy increases.
Resegregate	All three classes of Blacks constrain the rate at which intermarrying occurs (weighted effect); while more in number, resegregated Blacks (alone) have an unchanged ("Do Nothing") rate of life expectancy improvement.

---

[28] See Vernelia Randall (2006), *Dying While Black*, Seven Principles Press, Dayton, OH.

Diaspora	Upper-middle class population emigrate abroad (weighted effect); Blacks (alone) are fewer in number and experience a slower pace of life expectancy increases.
Nation Formation	Lower-middle and lower class population relocates outside of the U.S. in 2050 guided by a small *intelligencia* of upper-middle class Blacks (weighted effect); the loss of lower echelon Blacks causes life expectancy to exist at a higher level for those Blacks that remain because they are likely to be more attentive to proper healthcare.

Figure 9.—Life expectancy in the "53" paradigm

We estimate the "Do Nothing Series" by growing the 2010 life expectancy for males and females (70.2 and 77.2 years, respectively) by the average annual increase that has been exhibited by Black males and females over the 1980-2007 period (0.0034 and 0.0021 years, respectively).[29] The "Accelerate Integration" series is estimated by assuming that the loss of mixed-race (light-skinned) Blacks reduce life expectancy by an annual percentage that is equal to the number of the mixed-race population as a percentage of "Do Nothing" population. We adopt an identical annual pattern of life expectancy improvement for the "Resegregate" series as for the "Do Nothing" series because Black (alone) are added to the population, but do not affect the rate at which healthcare is obtained or life expectancy. For the "Diaspora" series, we reduce life expectancy that is reflected in the "Do Nothing" series by

---

[29] The data on life expectancy (1980-2007 estimates and a 2010 forecast) are published by the Census Bureau (http://www.census.gov/compendia/statab/2011/tables/11s0 103.pdf); however, the statistics are derived by U.S. National Center for Health Statistics.

the percentage of the upper-echelon Black population that is assumed to depart the U.S.—i.e., the percentage of the "Diaspora" to the "Do Nothing" population. For the "Nation Formation" series we boost the "Do Nothing" life expectancy by 10% to reflect a loss of mainly Blacks with poorer healthcare backgrounds, which permits the life expectancy to rise for the Afrodescendants who remain. Tables 7 and 8 present life expectancy forecasts for Black males and females, respectively.

Table 7.—Life Expectancy in Years, 2010-2050 (Males)

Action Scenario	2010	2020	2030	2040	2050
Do Nothing	70.2	72.7	75.2	77.8	80.5
Accelerate Integration	70.2	72.6	75.1	77.7	80.2
Resegregate	70.2	72.7	75.2	77.8	80.5
Diaspora	70.2	72.6	75.1	77.7	80.3
Nation Formation	70.2	72.7	75.2	77.8	88.6

Table 8.—Life Expectancy in Years, 2010-2050 (Females)

Action Scenario	2010	2020	2030	2040	2050
Do Nothing	77.2	78.9	80.6	82.3	84.1
Accelerate Integration	77.2	78.9	80.5	82.2	83.9
Resegregate	77.2	78.9	80.6	82.3	84.1
Diaspora	77.2	78.9	80.5	82.2	83.9
Nation Formation	77.2	78.9	80.6	82.3	92.5

Besides the "Nation Formation" strategy, Tables 7 and 8 reveal that the best-case scenarios out to 2050 are for Black American males and females to adopt a "Do Nothing" or a "Resegregate" strategy.

We should keep in mind that increased life expectancy can be valuable if the quality of life during the golden years is high because our elders can play key roles in imparting their knowledge and wisdom to younger generations. They can aid the youth in avoiding serious mistakes as they mature. Probably most importantly, our elders can serve as a source of roots for the very young so that they can see, in part, from whence they came.

Summary

All of the foregoing analysis was required to bring us to this summary. We wanted to determine which of the five action scenarios would produce the best outcomes for Black Americans by the time we reach 2050. Table 9 provides the top (most favorable) outcomes for Black Americans at the 2050 point.

Table 9.—"Best-Case" (Most Favorable) Scenarios

Variable	Values	Scenarios
Population (Millions)	63.2	Resegregate
Employment (Millions)	28.2	Resegregate
Income ($s Thousands)	105.7	Nation Formation
Entrepreneurship (Thousands)	11,092	Resegregate
Average Years of Schooling	16.45	Nation Formation
Incarceration (Thousands)	1,258	Nation Formation
Life Expectancy (Years)		
Males	88.6	Nation Formation
Females	92.5	Nation Formation

Table 9 shows that the "Resegregation" and "Nation Formation" scenarios predominate when it comes to producing the most "favorable" results. At a minimum, this information tells us that there are better alternatives for Black Americans than the status quo, and that what we need is a plan for change that can be implemented successfully. As might be expected, the most difficult aspects of the change process are: Coming together on which scenario(s) to adopt; agreement on a strategy; and identifying the appropriate enforcement and review practices that will lead to successful implementation and completion of the strategy.

If, on the other hand, Afrodescendants remain unorganized and choose to "Do Nothing," then Table 10 provides statistics on the likely outcomes.

Table 10.—"Do Nothing" Scenarios

Variable	Do Nothing Scenario
Population (Millions)	60.1
Employment (Millions)	26.2
Income ($s Thousands)	96.1
Entrepreneurship (Thousands)	10,644
Average Years of Schooling	14.96
Incarceration (Thousands)	1,398
Life Expectancy (Years)	
Males	80.5
Females	84.1

Table 11 identifies the difference between the best-case and "Do Nothing" strategies in percentage terms.

Table 11.—Performance Gap: Best-Case versus "Do Nothing" Scenarios

Variable	Percentage Difference Best-Case vs. Do Nothing
Population (Millions)	5.1%
Employment (Millions)	7.6%
Income ($s Thousands)	9.9%
Entrepreneurship (Thousands)	4.2%
Average Years of Schooling	9.9%
Incarceration (Thousands)	10.1%
Life Expectancy (Years)	
Males	10.0%
Females	9.9%

What we see is that a choice to analyze prospective outcomes and make a choice to change and improve those outcomes can be quite rewarding. Table 11 shows that the smallest improvement incurred from changing the status quo ("Do Nothing") occurs for entrepreneurship (4.2%) by adopting a "Resegregate" scenario. The question remains: Who can come along and convince Afrodescendants that it is in our best interest to change to become shapers, as opposed to victims, of history?

Let us close this chapter and this monograph by highlighting the fact that, although we have identified scenarios that can produce favorable outcomes over the "Do Nothing" strategy, our analysis purposefully fails to compare the state of Black America in 2050 with outcomes for White Americans. Something about which we can be assured, White Americans will not stand by idly and see conditions improving for Black Americans without taking the necessary action to maintain a superior distance between themselves and Afrodescendants.

This latter outcome should cause Black Americans to see that no matter which strategy is adopted to improve conditions, Afrodescendants are very likely to not improve dramatically their relative position vis-à-vis White Americans by the year 2050. In other words, there is a high probability that Black Americans are not likely to make substantial headway in creating the "equality" with White Americans that so many of Blacks seek.

On the other hand, those Black Americans who decide to call elsewhere home may not enjoy the outcomes that their brothers and sisters who remain in the U.S. enjoy in 2050. However, the former will be clear of the inequality consideration, and they can hold out a bright hope for rising to the highest heights in the generations to come, while their brothers and sisters who remain in the U.S. will remain constrained.

Note:
Complete 2010-2050 forecasted time series for each variable analyzed in Chapter 3 are available from the author upon request;
BlackEconomics@BlackEconomics.org; 808.232.7363.

Chapter 4.—Conclusion

As noted in the introduction, we have prepared no conclusion for this book. The conclusion must be written by those Afrodescendants who take a "Do Nothing" or other approach to writing the future history of our people in the Americas.

Index